Brian Urlacher

By Jeff Savage

AMAZING ATHLETES

Lerner Publications Company • Minneapolis

Lerner Publications Company
A division of Lerner Publishing Group, Inc.
241 First Avenue North
Minneapolis, MN 55401 U.S.A.

Website address: www.lernerbooks.com

Library of Congress Cataloging-in-Publication Data

Savage, Jeff, 1961–
     Brian Urlacher / by Jeff Savage.
          p.   cm. — (Amazing athletes)
     Includes bibliographical references and index.
     ISBN 978–0–8225–9991–3 (lib. bdg. : alk. paper)
     1. Urlacher, Brian—Juvenile literature. 2. Football players—United States—Biography—Juvenile literature. I. Title.
GV939.U76S38 2010
796.332092—dc22 [B]   2008053575

Manufactured in the United States of America
1 2 3 4 5 6 – BP – 15 14 13 12 11 10

TABLE OF CONTENTS

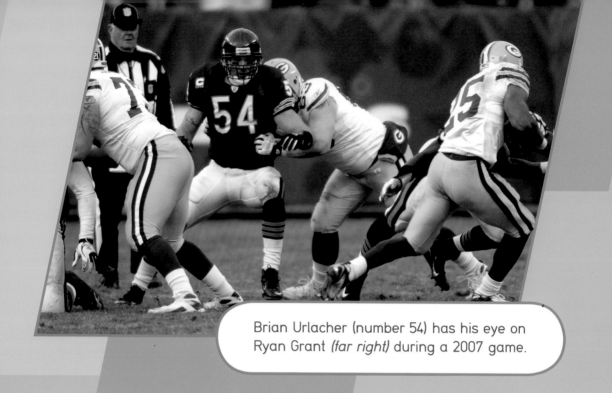

Brian Urlacher (number 54) has his eye on Ryan Grant *(far right)* during a 2007 game.

A GREAT RETURN

Brian Urlacher saw **running back** Ryan Grant headed his way. Brian lowered his shoulders and smacked into Grant. Brian wrapped his arms around him and drove him into the frozen turf. Brian's Chicago Bears were playing a 2007 game at snowy Soldier Field in Chicago against the rival Green Bay Packers.

Brian is a captain of one of the fiercest **defenses** in the National Football League (NFL). He plays **middle linebacker** with passion and force. He runs from across the field to chase down ball carriers. He slams opponents to the ground. After each play, he doesn't celebrate. He simply lines up and gets ready to defend again.

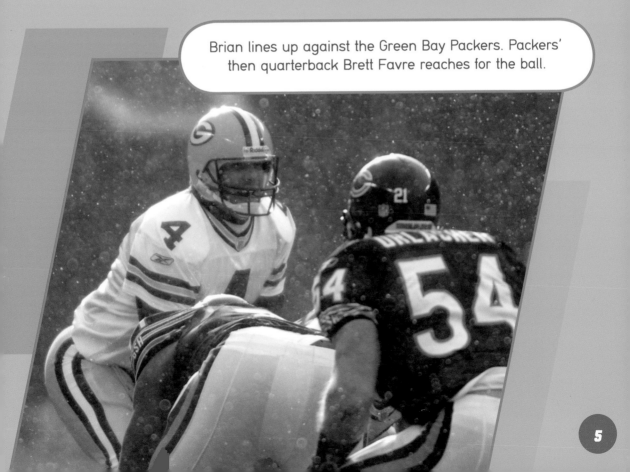

Brian lines up against the Green Bay Packers. Packers' then quarterback Brett Favre reaches for the ball.

Brian and the defense worked hard to stop the Packer offense.

The Bears had struggled through the 2007 season. With a 5–9 record, they were about to miss the **playoffs**. Meanwhile, the Packers were 12–2. They had one of the best records in the NFL.

But Brian wanted to prove his team could stop the Packers. The Bears defense forced the Packers to turn over the ball. The Bears offense took advantage. By the fourth quarter, the score was 28–7.

The Packers were frustrated. Early in the fourth quarter, they moved the ball down the field. Brian saw a short pass coming his way aimed at **wide receiver** Donald Driver. Brian stepped in front of Driver and batted the ball with his right arm. He tipped the ball to himself and caught it with his left hand. **Interception!** Brian took off. The Packers couldn't catch him. Brian rumbled 85 yards to the **end zone**. This was the first time he had returned an interception for a **touchdown** as an NFL player. The Bears won 35–7.

Brian *(right)* celebrates his touchdown.

Brian knew the win wouldn't change the Bears' losing season. Even so, he smiled as he walked off the field. Hundreds of fans were wearing his number 54 football jersey.

"It's just exciting to see all those '54' jerseys out there in the stands," said Brian. "It's crazy how people have taken to me."

Brian Urlacher is one of the most popular Bears' players ever. He's been named to the **Pro Bowl** six times. But fans in 2008 wondered if he still had the drive to help his team have a winning season. Would the Bears get into the playoffs in 2009?

Brian's family moved to Lovington, New Mexico, when he was eight. This picture shows Lovington High School's football field.

WORKING HARD

Brian Keith Urlacher was born May 25, 1978, in Pasco, Washington. Brian's mother, Lavoyda, and father, Brad, divorced when Brian was young. In 1986, Lavoyda took Brian and his older sister, Sheri, and younger brother, Casey, with her to Lovington, New Mexico. Lavoyda had grown up there. Brian's mom worked three jobs to support the family.

Brian's last name rhymes with linebacker.

In 1992, when Brian was 14, his mother married Troy Leonard. He became Brian's stepfather. "Brian didn't have much as a kid," said Brandon Ridenour, Brian's best friend. "His family lived paycheck to paycheck. Every role model he has ever had has been a hardworking type."

Brian liked playing sports and exercising. He worked out at a local gym. That same year, he joined the Wildcats, the football team at Lovington High. Coach Speedy Faith made Brian a wide receiver. Brian was five foot nine and weighed 160 pounds. To have a future in football, he knew he had to get bigger. He began **strength training**. He awoke every morning at five thirty. He and Casey rushed to the high school weight room. Brian focused on leg exercises. In two years, he bulked up to 210 pounds. He also grew to six foot four.

In 1995, as a senior, Brian was a scoring machine. He caught 61 passes for 15 touchdowns. He scored eight more on rushes and **punt** and **kickoff** returns. He led the Wildcats to a 14–0 record and the state title. In 1996, the University of New Mexico gave him a football **scholarship**. He'd switch from the Wildcats to the Lobos!

Brian was a standout player at Lovington.

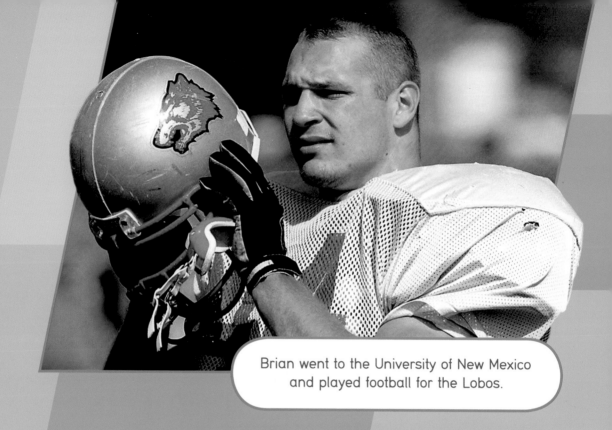

Brian went to the University of New Mexico and played football for the Lobos.

LOBO BACK

Brian sat on the bench in his first year at the University of New Mexico. He used the time to work hard in the weight room. By 1997, he weighed 235. He had packed on 25 pounds of muscle. That year, he got a bit more time on the field. Mostly, he played **free safety**.

In 1998, Rocky Long became New Mexico's new coach. He created a special position for Brian. It was called Lobo Back. Brian was free to play anywhere on defense. His job was to fly like a missile to the ball carrier. As a result, Brian recorded 178 tackles to lead the nation!

Coach Rocky Long *(below)* gave Brian a special job on defense.

Brian also played wide receiver on offense and returned kickoffs and punts. He was sensational as a senior. He finished his college career in 2000 with 442 career tackles to rank third all-time in Lobos' history. He had three interceptions, 11 **sacks**, and 11 **forced fumbles**. He averaged more than 15 yards on punt returns. Of his seven catches at wide receiver, six went for touchdowns!

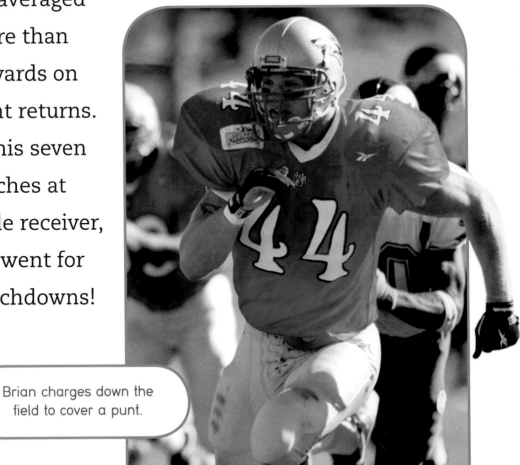

Brian charges down the field to cover a punt.

Brian's coaches taught him to be confident but never to boast. "It was important to Brian for the focus to be on the team," said assistant coach Mark Parks. "He didn't want it to be the Brian Urlacher Show."

Brian was ready for the pros. At the 2000 NFL **draft**, the Chicago Bears selected him with the ninth overall pick. Brian was thrilled. The Bears had a history of having outstanding linebackers. Could Brian compare to such legends?

Brian is often compared to three legendary Bears' linebackers: Bill George, Dick Butkus, and Mike Singletary.

Brian lines up during his first game starting as a middle linebacker in 2000.

"URLACHER 54"

Brian started for the Bears at **outside linebacker**. At first, he struggled. "For the most part, I'm lost," he said. "Everything is so much faster." For the third game of the season, coach Dick Jauron switched Brian to middle linebacker. It was a smart move. Brian made 13 tackles against the New York Giants. He also got his first quarterback sack.

During the 2000 season, Brian got more comfortable in his new position in the middle of the defense. He made 15 tackles and a sack against the New Orleans Saints. He got 11 tackles and two sacks against the Minnesota Vikings. For the season, Brian wound up leading the Bears in tackles with 124. He was named NFL Defensive Rookie of the Year and selected to the Pro Bowl for the first time.

In the NFL, team leaders often give post-season gifts to top performers. Brian rewarded each of his defensive linemen with a Rolex watch after his first season.

Brian leaps to tackle Vikings' running back Michael Bennett during a 2001 game.

Brian's second season was even better. The Bears defense allowed an NFL-low 203 points in 16 games. They kept two opponents from scoring at all. Brian finished with 148 tackles, six sacks, and three interceptions. He also scored two touchdowns. Against the Atlanta Falcons, Brian sacked Michael Vick, forced a fumble, and raced 90 yards for a touchdown! Against the Washington Redskins, he caught a pass on a fake field goal try and rumbled

27 yards for a score to win it 20–15. The Bears recorded a 13–3 record but were upset in the playoffs by the Philadelphia Eagles.

Brian had become like a coach on the field. He called out the signals for the defense. "I'm getting the call from the sideline, trying to get all the guys back to the huddle, trying to get them all on the same page. It's chaos!" Fans at Soldier Field in Chicago admired Brian's toughness. He played bare-armed even in the coldest games. He wore no jewelry. He did not dance or trash-talk. He just stopped opponents cold.

Bears fans like Brian's tough defensive play—even in bad weather.

In 2002, Brian led the league in tackles with 214. It shattered the Chicago all-time record of 190 set by Dick Butkus. Even though the Bears had a losing season, Brian was voted to his third straight Pro Bowl. The Urlacher 54 jersey became the most popular souvenir in the NFL.

Brian is often compared to Hall of Fame linebacker Dick Butkus. Butkus played for the Bears from 1965 to 1973.

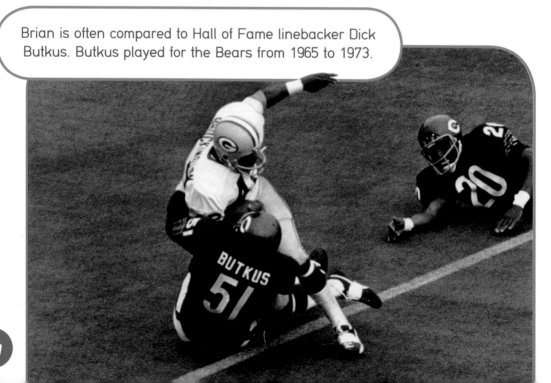

Some of Brian's fans wait to get his autograph outside a summer practice.

Brian was valuable to the Bears. They signed him to a nine-year **contract** worth more than $56 million. Brian earned millions more by appearing in commercials. He was happy to donate a lot of money to good causes. He bought 50 tickets for every Bears home game and gave them to children from the Special Olympics. He supplied Lovington High School with strength training equipment and shoes for athletes of every sport.

Brian led the Bears in tackles again in 2003, becoming the first Chicago player to lead the team his first four years. But the Bears suffered their second straight losing season. Jauron was fired, and Lovie Smith was named the new Bears coach. At first, the change didn't help. In 2004, the Bears finished 5–11. Brian suffered a leg injury and missed seven games. It snapped his streak of 64 straight starts at middle linebacker. Brian was frustrated.

Brian sits on the sidelines. An injury in a 2004 game against the Green Bay Packers kept him out of the game.

Brian tackles running back Noah Herron during the Bears' 2005 Christmas Day victory over the Green Bay Packers.

REACHING THE TOP

The Bears started the 2005 season slowly. By the fifth week, they had a 1–3 record. But Brian refused to give up. He rallied his defense, and the team won eight straight games. They clinched a playoff game by beating the Green Bay Packers on Christmas Day. The Bears allowed just 202 points on the season, the lowest in the league.

Brian led the charge with 171 tackles and six sacks. He was named Associated Press NFL Defensive Player of the Year. Mike Singletary is the only other Bears defender to receive the honor. The season ended with a thud when the Carolina Panthers shocked the Bears at home in the playoffs, beating the Bears 29–21.

Brian hoped to lead his team farther in 2006. He overcame a painful toe injury to carry the Bears to a 38–20 win over the New York Giants. He intercepted a pass in the

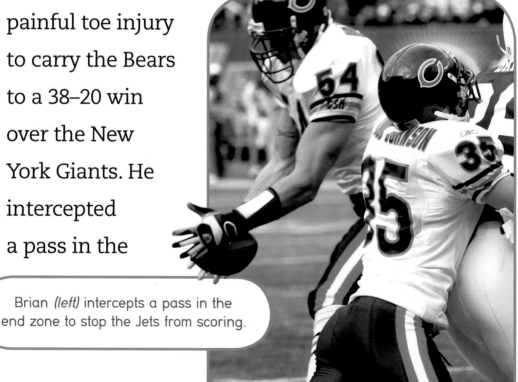

Brian *(left)* intercepts a pass in the end zone to stop the Jets from scoring.

end zone to preserve a shutout against the New York Jets. The Bears raced to a 7–0 record and finished 13–3.

This time, the team excelled in the playoffs. They edged the Seattle Seahawks, 27–24, in overtime. The next week, in the sleet and snow at Soldier Field, they throttled the New Orleans Saints, 39–14. The Bears had won the NFC Championship and were headed to the **Super Bowl**! But in Miami, Florida, for Super Bowl XLI, the Bears couldn't stop Peyton Manning and the Indianapolis Colts. The Bears' season ended with a 29–17 loss.

Brian lines up against Peyton Manning and the Indianapolis Colts in Super Bowl XLI.

Poor play, lots of injuries, and problems on offense and defense hurt the team in 2007 and 2008. The Bears missed the playoffs both years. Brian wasn't named to the Pro Bowl in either year. Some questioned whether Brian was a top-notch linebacker anymore. He believes he still can be a threat. The team's owners and coaches agree. They stretched his contract to keep him on the team through 2012.

No matter what the score is, Brian keeps the defense focused when it is on the field. At practices, Brian lets out belly laughs and keeps his teammates smiling. Most of all, he hustles when he is supposed to. Brian is determined to get the Bears back to the Super Bowl.

Brian *(second from right)* huddles with his teammates during a 2008 game.

In the meantime, Brian is having fun acting like a big kid. He invites his Bears teammates to his home in Chicago. They compete in paintball battles in his wooded backyard. They play cards, Ping-Pong, and air hockey.

Although his marriage ended in divorce, Brian takes his job as a parent seriously. For fun, he brings his daughters, Pamela and Riley, and his son, Kennedy, to Chuck E. Cheese's. They play games and eat pizza. Brian also supports several charities.

Brian is involved with the Special Olympics and the Ronald McDonald House.

For kids interested in football, Brian has this advice. "Just work hard and be smart," he says. "There is no real secret to it. If you are a good athlete, if you can play, they'll find you."

Selected Career Highlights

2008 Had career high four fumble recoveries
Finished second in team tackles

2007 Led Bears in team tackles for
seventh time
Had career high five interceptions

2006 Led Bears in team tackles for sixth time
Selected to Pro Bowl for sixth time

2005 Named Associated Press NFL Defensive Player
of the Year
Led Bears in tackles for fifth time
Selected to Pro Bowl for fifth time

2003 Set team record by leading Bears in tackles
for fourth straight year
Selected to Pro Bowl for fourth time

2002 Broke Bears all-time record for team tackles in single season (214)
Led the Bears in tackles for third straight year
Selected to Pro Bowl for third time

2001 Named *Football Digest* NFL Defensive Player of the Year
Finished fifth in the NFL Most Valuable Player voting
Led the Bears in tackles for second straight year
Selected to Pro Bowl for second time

2000 Led the Bears in tackles
Named Associated Press NFL Defensive Rookie of the Year
Selected to Pro Bowl for first time

1999 Named Associated Press first-team All-America
Name Mountain West Conference Player of the Year
Named first-team All-Mountain West Conference

1998 Named first-team All-Mountain West Conference

1995 Named prep First-team New Mexico All-State at wide receiver and
free safety

Glossary

contract: a written deal agreed to by a player and a team or a company

defense: the team of eleven players that doesn't have the football. The defense tries to stop the other team from scoring.

draft: a yearly event in which all professional teams in a sport take turns choosing new players from a selected group

end zone: the area beyond the goal line at each end of the field. A team scores a touchdown when it reaches the other team's end zone.

forced fumble: a play made by a defensive player that causes the ball carrier to lose possession of the ball

free safety: the defensive player who plays deep to help cover wide receivers and tackle ball carriers who break free

interception: a pass caught by a player on the defense. An interception results in the opposing team getting control of the ball.

kickoff: a kick of the ball that puts the football into play

middle linebacker: the player who stands behind the defensive linemen in the center of the field. This player calls plays for the defense.

outside linebacker: one of two defensive players who stand on either side of the middle linebacker

playoffs: a series of contests played after the regular season has ended

Pro Bowl: a game held every year after the season in which the best NFL players compete

punt: a kicked ball, usually on fourth down, that gives the other team the ball

running back: a player whose job is to run with the ball

sack: tackling the quarterback before he can throw or hand off the ball

scholarship: money awarded a student to help pay the costs of college

strength training: a workout routine performed with machines and weights that increases a person's strength

Super Bowl: the final game of each season between the champions of the American Football Conference (AFC) and the National Football Conference (NFC). The winner of the Super Bowl is that season's NFL champion.

touchdown: a score in which the team with the ball gets into the other team's end zone

wide receiver: a player who catches passes, mainly for a big gainFurther

Reading & Websites

Sandler, Michael. *Brian Urlacher.* New York: Bearport Press, 2009.

Savage, Jeff. *Peyton Manning.* Minneapolis: Lerner Publications Company, 2008.

Stewart, Mark. *The Chicago Bears.* Chicago: Northwood House Press, 2007.

Uschan, Michael V. *Brian Urlacher.* Broomall, PA: Mason Crest, 2008.

Brian Urlacher's Official Website
http://www. brianurlacher.com
This is Brian's official website, featuring a biography, news, photos, statistics, and information about Brian's charity work.

Chicago Bears: The Official Site
http://www.nfl.com/teams/chicagobears
The official website of the Chicago Bears that includes the team schedule and results, late-breaking news, biographies of Brian Urlacher and other players and coaches, and much more.

Sports Illustrated Kids
http://www.sikids.com
The *Sports Illustrated Kids* website covers all sports, including football.

Index

Photo Acknowledgments

The images in this book are used with the permission of: © Warren
Wimmer/Icon SMI, pp. 4, 5, 6; AP Photo/Nam Y. Huh, p. 7; AP Photo/Jake
Schoellkopf, pp. 9, 14; Seth Poppel Yearbook Library, p. 11; AP Photo/
Albuquerque Journal, Jim Thompson, p. 12; AP Photo/Albuquerque Journal,
Kitty Clark, p. 13; © Jonathan Daniel/Allsport/Getty Images, pp. 16, 18; AP
Photo/Keith Srakocic, p. 19; AP Photo, p. 20; AP Photo/Ted S. Warren, p. 21;
© Scott Boehm/Getty Images, p. 22; AP Photo/Mike Roemer, p. 23; © Jeff
Zelevansky/Icon SMI, p. 24; AP Photo/Jeff Roberson, p. 25; © Kevin C. Cox/
NFL/Getty Images, p. 26; © Wesley Hitt/Getty Images, p. 27; © David Stluka/
Getty Images, p. 29.

Front Cover: © Jonathan Daniel/Getty Images.